HORSES

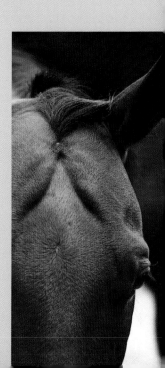

HORSES

BY JAY DUSARD

ESSAYS BY THOMAS McGUANE

RIO NUEVO PUBLISHERS
Tucson, Arizona

To my wife, Kathie, horsewoman and healer

—J. D.

Rio Nuevo Publishers®
P.O. Box 5250, Tucson, Arizona 85703-0250
(520) 623-9558, www.rionuevo.com

Design: Karen Schober, Seattle, Washington
Endsheets image: *Escaramuza*. Sketch used on pages 14, 42, and 66 is by Maynard Dixon, pencil on paper.

Library of Congress Cataloging-in-Publication Data

Dusard, Jay.
  Horses / by Jay Dusard ; essays by Thomas McGuane.
     p. cm.
  ISBN 1-887896-77-5 (hardcover)
  ISBN-13: 978-1-887896-77-1 (hardcover)
  1. Horses--United States--Anecdotes. 2. Horses--United States--
Pictorial works. 3. McGuane, Thomas. I. McGuane, Thomas. II. Title.
  SF301.D87 2005
  636.1'0022'2--dc22
                                    2005000946

Printed in Hong Kong
10 9 8 7 6 5 4 3 2 1

THERE ARE FEW THINGS MORE EXCITING THAN RELEASING A BAND OF YOUNG HORSES FROM A

CORRAL WHERE THEY HAVE BEEN CONFINED FOR SOME TIME INTO OPEN SPACE AND WATCHING

THE EXPLOSION OF MOVEMENT AS THESE METEORS TAKE ON OPEN COUNTRY.

—THOMAS McGUANE

Overleaf: Un Desfile de los Charros.

CONTENTS

PART ONE **HORSES THROUGH THE LENS** 14

PART TWO **HORSES** 42

PART THREE **A FOAL** 66

Overleaf: Joe Launderville with Belgian Team, Grant-Kohrs Ranch, Montana.

HORSES, BLESS 'EM ALL, HAVE KEPT ME BROKE, FRUSTRATED, IN AWE, AND IN LOVE.

—JAY DUSARD

I DIDN'T GROW UP AROUND HORSES, but dang sure wish I had. I grew up between corn and soybean rows in southern Illinois, and big red Farmall tractors were my mounts. I coveted the dandy little paint mare that one neighbor kid had. No matter how hard I whipped, my balloon-tired bicycle couldn't keep up with her.

HORSES THROUGH THE LENS

I bought my first horse, a four-year-old Texas buckskin, in 1962 and have been hauling hay and shoveling ever since. I was in the peacetime army at the time I bought Buck and started punching cows in my free time with rancher friends who ran their stock on the Fort Hood reservation. Upon discharge, and eminently unqualified, I lucked into a cowboying job on a wonderful family-run ranch in southeastern Arizona—a life-altering experience that I have never outgrown.

My attraction to and involvement with horses is well into its fifth decade, with no end in sight. I have been privileged to log countless backroad miles throughout North America, photographing the men and women who make their living on horseback. Much of this time I've worked in black-and-white, in large format and more recently in medium format, but all along the trail I've made 35-mm color shots, and I've done a stretch or two of 35-mm black-and-white shooting.

Everything you see here is from and of the West, the region that rocks my soul. This volume is ranch oriented, so it falls short of representing all riding disciplines and all equine breeds. My admiration for mules and burros shows up, however.

Horses, bless 'em all, have kept me broke, frustrated, in awe, and in love.

THE HORSE WORLD ABOUNDS with contests. Racing, jumping, dressage, driving, pulling, *pato*, polo, cross-country, endurance, *buzkashi*, jousting, vaulting, cutting, penning, barrel racing, bronc riding … the beat goes on.

Industry is not known for spawning major sports, but Mexican *charrería* and its American counterpart, rodeo, are clearly derived from the range cattle business. The timeclock that is so fundamental to rodeo is largely absent from the colorful, highly traditional *charreada*. Style, a significant factor, of course, in American bronc and bull riding, is of overriding importance in most of the Mexican *suertes*, or competitive events, and especially in the roping events, some with the roper mounted, some with him on foot. Within a generous time limit, the most difficult, flowery, and intricate loops that "connect" are the ones the judges score the highest. *Escaramuza* is the mid-performance spectacle

performed by a team of eight young women, the *adelitas*, riding sidesaddle and executing complex quadrille maneuvers at blazing speed.

Working cowboy rodeo is what you see in this book, not professional or any of the other more popular versions of the sport. The bronc riding is handled in the original pre-bucking chute manner. In the arena, the bronc is snubbed up to a gentle saddle horse. The contestant cinches on his working saddle and mounts over the back of the snubbin' horse. Then … let the dance begin!

HAVING OWNED MY FIRST HORSE for over a year and having dabbled in rodeo-style calf roping, it followed that the next step should be to try my hand at bareback bronc riding. My rodeo initiation took place in Fort Smith, Arkansas, in the spring of 1963. A local stock contractor needed to audition some bucking horse prospects, so he put out the word for riders. Being male, ambulatory, and in possession of a bareback riggin' were the only requirements, so even this greenhorn passed muster. No entry fee, no prize money, three head per customer.

From the middle of bronc number one, I zeroed in on his ears and nodded for the gate. My sorrel made a quick sashay to the left, and I plummeted down between his feet. I rolled into a ball to avoid the

Trick Roping Practice.

Saddle-Bronc Riding, Arizona Cowpunchers Reunion.

massive, whizzing, untrimmed hooves as he bucked over me into the arena.

"Are you sure you want to go through with this, kid?" sighed Mister Stock Contractor from somewhere up above.

"Yes, sir. I'll do better on the next one."

By the time I came around again in the rotation, my chagrin was transformed into resolve. *Número dos* was a dun, and I was ready. I rared back, asked for him, and turned on the spur-lick I had perfected on a couple of logging mules one day near Fort Polk, Louisiana. In perfect rhythm and way down the arena, here I was, winnin' the West and makin' it look plumb easy. Then, my zebra dun ducked off to the right, and yours truly kept going straight, hearing the splat just before the eight-second buzzer.

From low down again, I studied the surface of the arena, marveling at how its slablike precision had scarcely been defiled by the once-over of tractor and disk. I felt myself being hoisted upwards by my armpits and transported back uprange. The cowboy on the right was four feet wide and all muscle; the guy on the left was smaller and asked if he could have my third bronc.

"No!"

Bronco three was a paint, and I was hurtin'. What I perfected on this go-round was a relatively soft landing at four, maybe five seconds into the mission.

The warm flush I felt as I hauled my carcass into the white GMC pickup that would soon take me irretrievably westward came from more than a considerably bruised left gluteus. The glow diminished quickly, but there's a little warm spot left, somewhere between myth and memory.

I SAVORED BEING HORSEBACK every day during that cowboying job later in 1963, when I had the good fortune to live and work on the old John Slaughter Ranch, now the Malpai Ranch. The ranch lies on the Arizona-Sonora border in the midst of a vast volcanic field, complete with cinder cones, craters, and lava flows. The basaltic rock is known locally as malpai, from the Spanish *mal país*, meaning bad country.

A cattle trader had made a deal with owners Warner and Wendy Glenn to pasture 347 head of Mexican steers on the Malpai. Some of these steers were inclined to wander and would crawl through the fence onto the neighboring Bar M Ranch.

One day Warner got word that two of the steers were luxuriating on Bar M grass. Too late that afternoon he and I trotted the several miles to the target area. Deep in the indicated pasture, in the twilight, we found them—one solid black and one black with a wide, white belt. On the drive back the two miscreants kept splitting up—requiring us to follow suit. A thunderstorm had rolled in, drenching us and making the moonless night seem a full f/stop darker than black. Warner and I kept track of each other during the lightning flashes and by the sparks struck by steel horseshoes on malpai rock.

My steer, by the luck of the draw the solid black, decided to climb the big cinder hill we had intended to bypass. Maybe halfway up I lost track of him. During one particularly bright series of flashes I made careful note of the surroundings, then urged Buck in the direction I was positive the steer had taken. Buck didn't want to untrack, but I insisted, first with legs, then with spurs. We struggled with each other for endless minutes, over the boulders and through the brush, until Buck became an absolutely immovable object. The next lightning flashes revealed that we were in exactly the same spot where I had commenced my pounding. Also revealed was the black steer, partially hidden behind a mesquite bush.

Moral: never start an argument with your working partner. Especially one with superior night vision and a far better understanding of cow.

WHEN I FIRST WENT TO WORK on the ranch, I noticed a few mules in the horse pasture.

"We ride 'em on our hunts," explained Warner, who is a highly respected cougar hunter, tracker, and guide.

Soon a guided lion hunt came up and I was invited along to wrangle dudes and generally help out. One of the first things I noticed was how hard my good Texas buckskin had to work to keep up with the unflappable, efficient saddle mules on the steep mountain trails. On the second day of the hunt, Warner and his father, Marvin Glenn, decided to split the party. Marvin took the hunters, and I went with Warner, who was mounted on Mochomo, his venerable bay Mexican mule. Soon our dogs hit a lion track, and we loped along after them, reining up where the ridge ended in a steep jumble of boulders and bedrock.

"You'll never make it down here, much less keep up with this mule," Warner allowed.

"No kiddin'," I agreed.

He pointed out a rendezvous spot deep in the canyon and with a cheery "See ya!" sent a barely discernible signal to Mochomo's ribcage via the rowels of his Chihuahua spurs.

Like a long-eared hang glider the mule leaped into the abyss, striking long trails of sparks with his shoes each time he caromed off another level of slickrock in his spectacular descent. In a matter of seconds he dropped completely out of sight, only to reappear at a high lope on a bench far below. At the end of the bench, and without breaking stride, Mochomo again propelled himself into deep space.

Gilberto Rivera and Francisco Carranza, Rancho El Diablo, Sonora, Mexico.

As Buck and I painstakingly worked our way down the alternate route, I simply marveled at what I had witnessed, replaying the delectable mind's-eye tape and grinning the grin of a true believer.

SOME FORTY YEARS AGO, a group of friends and I were ambushed by an intense summer rainstorm in the grassy San Rafael Valley near Patagonia, Arizona. Spread out in the deluge, we were crossing a high, open ridge when a bolt of lightning blasted the ground barely to the left of the borrowed gray mare my architect boss was riding. No harm, no foul!

So, we're back in camp, drying out and feeling lucky, when my buddy Dave Lewis observes, "Well, I guess it's true what the old-timers used to say in stormy weather."

"Oh?"

"Ride the bay and pack the gray."

SUMMER AGAIN, and my friend Gary Tuck and I were horseback in Redington Pass above Tucson. He was on the gray paint he'd recently traded for, and I was riding my bay thoroughbred, Scorpion. Heavy clouds moved in. Thunder started to roll, and so did Gary's eyes. Muttering something about gray horses attracting lightning, and dead cowboys, he whipped up and we were a-bookin' it through the cactus,

boulders, and slickrock in a beeline for the pickup and trailer.

Dead ahead: bright green T-posts, four strands of new barbed wire stretched to a high treble tuning, and no gates in sight. Instantly, Gary was afoot wielding fence pliers. Zing, zing, zing, zing!

"I know this is against the code," said he. "But I'll come back tomorrow and fix the son of a bitch."

At least he didn't offer me a horse trade.

SCORPION WAS BRED TO RUN. The three-year-old bay gelding was allegedly a thoroughbred, kinda small, but very refined. No Jockey Club papers were offered with the $300 price tag. No big deal for a sharp-looking gelding, however. The colt was said to go back to Fair Play, Man O'War's sire, but he hadn't come down through the illustrious "Big Red."

The colt had four black feet (I like that). In fact, his only "chrome" was a small white snip on the nose that could be construed to resemble a scorpion. Hence the name. Scorp had been started over at Tucson's Rillito race track—jockey broke. He'd been out of a starting gate but had never run a race.

I saddled my new acquisition, mounted him in an arena, and walked him all of thirty feet into a little bunch of calves. He immediately started nuzzling one, not biting, but just mouthing the critter along the spine

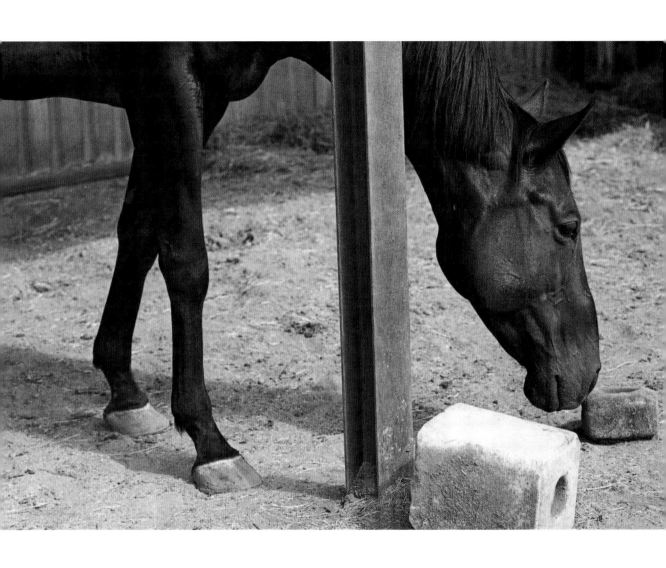

and up and down its hind legs. I directed Scorp to another calf, and he did the same thing. Then another calf. Same deal. He didn't sample them all, as I recall. What I delightedly realized was that he had forgotten about me and was completely focused on the bovines, most likely the first ones he'd ever seen.

I'd had my first horse, Buck, for only five years before I lost him at age nine to colic from possibly poisoned hay. Buck had endured my ham-handedness and lack of finesse, and in spite of me, had become a fairly good cowhorse. We became regulars at shows of the fledgling Southern Arizona Cutting Horse Association that my wife, Kathie, and I had helped to launch.

Now with Scorpion, thank God I was savvy enough to realize that I had a clean slate—that I should essentially leave him alone and let him train me. For the most part, I trusted him and managed not to goof him up. Riding with Warner Glenn at the Slaughter Ranch one day, Scorp in one jump launched me skyward, then waited in place to catch me perfectly centered in the saddle. Mutual trust, you might say.

Scorpion went on to make Kathie and me an exceptionally versatile horse. For all that we asked of him, he required virtually zero training. With English tack, he took Kathie over the jumps. He took me un-

erringly to the steer's heels in what little team roping I attempted. He had a terrific "handle"—self-taught, of course, with us simply trying to deliver correct, understandable cues. Outside or in corrals he was great to work cattle on. Plumb cowy, he made fantastic blocking moves, all on his own.

Sounds perfect, but he wasn't. When there was nothing for him to do but just stand around, he'd drive you nuts with his weaving, or his general nervousness. He'd try to scramble up the right side of the horse trailer on left turns that weren't taken at an absolute crawl. He needed a lot more honest work than a fundamentally disorganized photographer could give him.

We had moved to northern Arizona not long after I bought Scorpion. Away from any cutting horse activity in that place and time, he never did set foot in a cutting arena, never did compete for buckles and glory for his master.

He more than made up for this one day on the Toehold Ranch, run by fine cowman and cowboy deluxe Bob Murphy. We gathered some cattle and penned them in a remote set of corrals. Bob would sort out a cow and head her toward me, and my job was to drive her into the next pen and watch the open gate. I began to wonder what Scorp could do if some ol' cow just happened to turn back and bolt for the main bunch.

The footing in those corrals was terrible—uneven, sloping, hard-packed dirt the consistency of a rough concrete slab. Only a layer of ball bearings could have made it worse. So, naturally, I let a cow turn back and pitched ol' Scorp the slackest of reins.

That cow really tested my horse, but he expertly blocked every inside move and head fake she threw at him. Scorpion ran the show, and I was simply the enthralled onboard witness. The biggest part of me wanted this dance to go on forever, but the instant that cow "gave" a little, we turned her toward the next pen and drove her on.

Behind us I heard the normally taciturn Bob intone, "That horse will look at a cow."

IN 1981 I RECEIVED a Guggenheim fellowship to photograph the working cowboys of North America. This put me on the road in a new Datsun King Cab with a camper jam-packed with camera outfits, bedroll, saddle, and cowpunchin' gear. My first foray took me into southwestern Canada.

One late September afternoon on British Columbia's sprawling Gang Ranch, cow boss Lonnie Jones and I rode out from Big Meadow camp. The fall roundup was a week away, and our objective was to gather all the cattle we could from the grassy lake country called Fosbury. Spot and Spook, Lonnie's bor-

der collies, enthusiastically responding to shouted and hand signals, took care of the outermost sweeps, making fairly short work of our thousand-head-plus gather.

The sun, after hiding for several hours behind a thin but uniform cloud cover, had long since set. Leaving our herd to drift, we headed homeward through the coniferous "stick country," climbing through a fenced driveway, a murky, manmade tunnel, straight as a chalk line (an engineer's dream, a surveyor's nightmare), a curious, monotonous, conversation-spawning environment.

We emerged finally into a large space, Big Swamp by name. Low to starboard a sliver of new moon seemed powerless to do more than hint at its position behind the persisting veil of cloud. Softly lenticular shapes of timber floated in space, like islands in a misty sea, as the horses eagerly accepted our invitation to lope the subliminal trail entering the dream before us.

Tall Timber, my chunky blue roan mount, rolled solidly into the gloom. It was easy to pitch the old craftsman a slack rein and savor the trip as he outmaneuvered the grindstones, muskegs, and other boogers of the night that lay between him and the stack of sweet meadow hay at camp.

Out there afoot I would have been reduced to jelly. I imagined that Lonnie was smiling knowingly through the darkness.

Lonnie Jones, Gang Ranch, British Columbia, Canada.

Terry Milliken, Douglas Lake Cattle Co., British Columbia, Canada.

TERRY MILLIKEN'S REPUTATION in British Columbia was a good one. When I pulled into the headquarters of the Douglas Lake Cattle Co. and asked about him, I was sent to the quarter horse barn nearby.

I met Terry at the round corral, where he ran in a fabulous-looking registered bay filly. As she circled at a lope, suspicious but not scared, Terry's loop shot out in throat-latching perfection. Hobbled, talked to, gently rubbed and popped with the blanket, the mare seemed ready to accept the oncoming saddle. But just before the final tug at the latigo, she burst into a rampage of violent pitching and bawling. The blanket was the first item to take flight, then the saddle, finally the soft hobble rope—as they say in the West, the whole shitaree.

Terry regrouped, then resumed the lesson. He turned her loose with the saddle on so she could have it out with herself, kept her moving, turned her back, roped the saddle horn, ridding her (he hoped) of evil spirits with each lap around the bronc pen.

Caught again, her forefeet hobbled, and now with a snaffle bridle in place, the little mare was given further opportunity for reflection. After maybe five minutes, Terry quietly walked up to her, stepped into the left stirrup, and, holding the saddle horn with his right hand, gently pulled himself upward. His full weight was now being borne by the filly. He eased down, then back up, repeating the maneuver until she acceded to it.

Terry removed the hobbles and this time deftly swung all the way on. Summoning up her remaining wildness, the mare came absolutely unpuckered. She lurched forward, bogged her head, traded ends, and bellowing equine insults, repeatedly shot skyward, leaving her shadow far below her on the sand.

Milliken—the pro—dead center, no daylight, rode her through the big jumps, down through the smaller ones, and into an easy circling lope. He stopped her, moved her out at a trot, guided her around, elicited a couple of tasty first-saddle rollbacks, and in general had her settling down and going his way. A good horse hand.

WORKING, PLEASURE, and show horses are our captives. Since we expect so much of them, and they are so intrinsically willing to grant us our wishes, they deserve a great deal from us—often more than we civilians are savvy enough to give. Fortunately for horses, help is out there for civilians.

Kathie and I are old enough to have ridden as participants with the late Monte Foreman, the originator of the horsemanship clinic. Monte's experience as polo player, cavalryman, and cowboy, plus his drawings and film studies of horses in motion, evolved into the Horse Handling Science he presented so clearly. I've been privileged to ride lots of different horses in my photographic peregrinations among the cow outfits of western North America. And while nobody ever cut me out a widowmaker, I do credit Monte with giving me the keys to harmonizing with them all.

On the outfits I got acquainted with men like Terry Milliken, and Wade Cooper of the ZX in Oregon, who are still referred to as bronco men or roughstring riders but who operate in highly enlightened contrast to the "busters" and "bronc fighters" photographed a century earlier by L. A. Huffman.

My three days photographing and riding on Buster and Sheila Welch's ranch have to be my most memorable. Buster grew up cowboying on big west Texas outfits and brings this experience to the way he has revolutionized the training of cutting horses. For example, the young horses that he and his apprentices start and ride are engaged in the reality of cattle work on the range and in the branding corrals. They tend to enter the cutting pen with a good work ethic and some cow savvy, so they can be kept very natural in their training.

Sheila Varian lit up the Cow Palace in San Francisco back in 1961 when she piloted her Arabian mare, Ronteza, all the way to the title of Grand Champion Reined Cowhorse. Renowned for breeding and raising world-class Arabian horses, Sheila is also a leading exponent and practitioner of reining in the California vaquero tradition.

In 1997 I spent a week on location for the Redford/Disney production of *The Horse Whisperer*, photographing for the film's companion book. Buck Brannaman and Curt Pate, in addition to furnishing and handling horses, were the advisors who worked closely with Robert Redford, fine-tuning his horsemanship for the title role. Since that movie gig, I've been to a number of Buck's exceptionally fine horsemanship and ranch roping clinics.

For several winters, the Edsall family of Montana—Merle, Sharon, Roy, and Clayton—relocated their horse-training operation to southern Arizona, where their colt-starting and horsemanship clinics have truly benefitted the horses and riders of this region. In addition to sending our colts to the Edsalls for training, I rode our middle-aged stallion, Docs Juniper Dust, in a Joe Wolter cow-working clinic that they hosted.

Joe Wolter's excellent ranch-roping video shows his mentor, Bill Dorrance, well into his nineties, riding and throwing beautiful loops. I doubt if anyone has understood and respected horses more completely than have the late Dorrance brothers, Tom and Bill. They gave form, substance, and inspiration, especially through the outreach of the great clinician Ray Hunt, to today's best horse hands.

Sheila Varian and Lightly Bey V, Varian Arabians, California.

Departure, Spanish Ranch, Nevada.

"LOOKS LIKE YOU HAVE A BABY COMING fairly soon," said the veterinarian, looking at the Brahma cow in the pen.

"She'll have her calf tonight," said our friend Chris.

"No way, lady. Several days. Maybe a week. Just what makes you think she'll deliver tonight?"

"Gary, she's already been talking to her baby."

As they watched, the cow swung her head around to her belly and began a series of soft gruntlike utterances. "I'm so lucky to have a bovine psychologist like you for a client," said the vet, shaking his head and moving toward his pickup.

Curiosity brought the doc on a bit of a detour from the next morning's calls. In Chris's pen was a bright new heifer, licked clean and dry, lying at the feet of a doting mother.

MOONY, THE BIG SORREL MARE, was two weeks overdue and uncomfortable. She'd been ballooning, almost alarmingly, for weeks out in the big pasture with the other mares. Kathie and I had brought her into the barn right before her due date and kept tabs on the steady filling and tightening of her udder. After she'd started dripping milk, we'd gone on serious colt watch.

Around ten P.M. Moony was restless, moving back and forth from stall to paddock. Before long she started the hind-leg-to-belly kicks that indicate the onset of labor. As we watched and waited, she periodically looked back at her enormous belly.

Moony's always had a deep voice that sounds like an old Ford with a rusted-out muffler. We thought—then knew—that we were hearing it. Ever so softly, Moony's monologue, directed at her belly.

We began the drill: Pop a couple of bales and scatter clean straw throughout the stall. Bring the mare in. Slide the doors shut. Wait.

Moony's water broke, and with a groan, she eased herself down. More turning toward the belly and talking. And straining. The bubble appeared, like a prankster's water balloon. Then, inside the bubble, a foot pointing downward, then another foot, then a nose—all elements perfectly positioned. As the baby's head emerged incrementally with each of Moony's pushes, we helped by holding onto the legs and pulling gently until the shoulders were out. The rest of the young 'un slithered out with a rush.

Moony resumed her low nickering and was answered with a sharp whinny—the clarion call of her brand new filly. It was two A.M., and we were inclined to think it had been a dialogue all along.

WHEN YOU DRIVE EASTWARD from Tombstone toward McNeal, Arizona, you see on your right

Sam Redding and Ron Willis, Big Loop Rodeo, Oregon.

the Mule Mountains. Graceful and sweet, especially in late afternoon light, they rise out of the Sulphur Springs Valley in gentle undulations like the backgrounds in an early Disney animated film.

Don't let the velour fool you. They are rough, dirty boogers. The grassy slopes are absolutely covered with huge loose, jagged rocks, and the gentle looking gradients, when you and your mount are struggling to get above some rimmin' out cow-calf pair, are frighteningly steep. And taxing. The fresh horse that offered to buck you off at the outset will be plumb out of the notion. Getting back down toward the drive with a scattering of bovines that refuse to coalesce can be a game of agonizing three-dimensional chess. In all of your downhill back-and-forth, you may be afoot and leading at times. And when your saddle is on round-backed Luna's neck, and you're wishing that you'd rigged her up with a breeching, you'll step down and figure out that the best way to reset that heavy sucker is to point Luna back uphill. Gravity can be your friend.

All of the smallish mountain ranges in southeastern Cochise County, where my rancher friends run cows, look rougher than the Mules. They aren't; they're just less deceptive. This country can make the geologist in you think that vulcanism originated here.

The natural barefoot hoof trimming so popular these days will most likely serve your horse admirably in the East, and on the flats and even the mountain trails around here. But, if your intention is to punch cows in this neighborhood, you'd better see to it that Luna and Dunny and Circle and Spud are shod with iron.

IN PHOTOGRAPHING HORSES, the subject is sculpture. Sculpture that races, rests, fears, flees, fights, bucks, works and plays, lives, and dies. Nothing, in my estimation, is as sublimely beautiful as the horse—in any light, and almost any context.

Horses can be so beautiful that you begin to think that they can almost photograph themselves. All you have to do is point the camera and pull the trigger.

Not so. It is entirely possible—nay, easy as pie—to make Pegasus look like a hyena. Here's how. Grab almost any one-lens camera. Stand close enough to Peg's shoulder that he almost fills the frame, with his head near and hip far. Everything looks great, because you don't see the distortion that the lens "sees." The taller you are and the shorter the focal length of the lens, the greater the distortion. It's a matter of perspective, which is, without exception, a matter of lens-to-subject distance. A close viewpoint always results in a tremendous disparity of apparent size from front to back. That's how you make the perfectly conformed equine resemble the ungainly scavenger of the veldt.

To make all the parts of the horse appear in harmonious proportion, the photograph must be made from a more distant viewpoint. A lens of longer than normal focal length enables one to better fill the frame with the subject. A wide-angle or normal lens will see the same relationships from that same, more distant viewpoint. But the subject will be smaller, requiring considerable enlarging and cropping.

A horse and its rider are often photographed together—the equestrian portrait. The direct sunlight that enhances the muscle definition of the horse will create an abysmal shadow under the hatbrim of the rider—the Lone Ranger effect if the angle of the sun is relatively low, or the Hangman effect in the vicinity of high noon. In making equestrian images, if my prayers for cloud cover to diffuse the light and overcome the harsh shadows aren't answered, I invariably seek the shady side of a building, or trees with dense foliage.

As the ideal relationship between horse and rider is one of partnership, the relationship between photographer and human subject thrives on partnership. The person photographed should feel respected, willing, relaxed, and confident of the truth and authenticity of the result.

For years I have made rather formal black-and-white equestrian portraits with tripod-mounted 4x5-, 5x7-, and 8x10-inch view cameras. More recently, in order to streamline logistics and work with a bit more flexibility, I have begun using a 6x9-cm rollfilm camera, still on a tripod most of the time. Significantly, it turns out that the majority of the images in this book were made over the past quarter century with my little 35-mm "derringer," as color documentation of my rangeland adventures, along with a series of photographic details inspired by the sketches of favorite painters like Winslow Homer and Maynard Dixon.

Of the relatively few action images in this book, many, including the bucking horse and roping shots, were done with my early-model Olympus OM-1, with me advancing the film with my thumb and getting lucky. When Tom McGuane and I were assigned by *Texas Monthly* to do a story about the great cutting horse trainer Buster Welch, I borrowed a Nikon with a motor drive. This enabled me to shoot bursts of exposures, the only way to do justice to the spontaneous, unchoreographed ballet of horse and cow. My brand-new servo-driven auto-focus, multi-modal auto-exposure, rapid-advance film camera with zoom lenses and built-in flash that outthinks me so handily *should* be able to keep pace with a great cutting horse. I hope so.

Digital? I ain't there yet.

—JAY DUSARD

Buster Welch, Welch Ranch, Texas.

IT IS NOT THE DUTY OF THE HORSE TO BE A BIOFEEDBACK MECHANISM FOR YEARNING

HUMANS; YET IT IS REMARKABLE HOW CONSISTENTLY PEOPLE WITH HORSES CLAIM TO

HAVE LEARNED MUCH ABOUT THEMSELVES THROUGH THEM.

—*THOMAS McGUANE*

Overleaf: Burros at BLM Auction.

PART TWO

THOSE WHO LOVE HORSES are impelled by an ever-receding vision, some enchanted transformation through which the horse and the rider become a third, much greater thing. No such image haunts the dreams of the motorist. Becoming one with your car is the subject of perhaps unforeseen comedy. The dream of animals is counterpoised by the nightmare that our inventions will turn on us. This is the age of the machine and all things of flesh are imperiled by it,

HORSES

especially that terrible machine of transportation the automobile, which has ruined our towns, our countryside, and perhaps our families. The geopolitics of oil, the murderous disquiet of the oil-producing regions owe their unhappiness to the need to fuel that thing that replaced the horse. The humblest horse owner with a cherished animal in the back yard is doing his or her part to help the spirit travel in a more bountiful way.

Somehow, in the last thirty years, my life has filled up with horses and with other animals as well, dogs certainly, numerous barn cats, several wonderful cockatiels, the wild animals we live among, some of whom have become habituated to us. We are particularly aware of nearby annual nesters, the red-tailed hawks, the golden eagles, the all-knowing ravens, and the bird for

Merle, Clayton, and Sharon Edsall, Apache Springs Ranch, Arizona.

whom Montanans have an ironic and amused affection, the magpie. Animals seem to belong to a family from which only man is estranged.

I bought a small ranch in the 1960s and over the last several decades it has moved and enlarged. Living on a ranch was my choice but my four children simply grew up that way, going from one-room schools to the state university. Horses were always around, always, in the view of others, too many of them. Now the children are grown and gone but my wife and I are not alone. The horses are still here.

Horses occupy a special place because they require so much care, and because they are curiously fragile, possessing the prey species' excessive faith in the value of flight. A friend of mine in Oklahoma said to me, "God made a perfect world but he would like one chance to redesign the horse." Certainly, some work could be done with feet, hocks, suspensory tendons, navicular bones, all of which seem far too delicate for the speed and weight of the horse. And too often, the fifty feet of unsupported intestine acquires a simple loop and kills the horse. If the horse were a Ford, the species would vanish beneath lawsuits engendered by consumer-protection laws.

I've sometimes wondered why I've spent so much time with horses. In the past, I was quite happy with mice. I had several lovely ones. I see nearly as much in their pert whiskers and beady eyes as I do in million-dollar Northern Dancer yearlings. But because of its size, the horse imposes its moods and ways upon us. My wife and I have occasionally considered bringing our horses into the house so that they could see exactly where we live, but have declined out of concern that they would find some of our more doubtful possessions, our television, say, or the telephone, so alarming that they would express their disapproval by destroying furniture and walls. Who would blame them?

Size doesn't tell the whole story, but I've occasionally envied the East Indians whose lives are given to the care of elephants, whose size says something about the consent by animals to the very existence of the fast-breeding turbo-monkey called man. If you think of animals as humanity and mankind as the lawyers, you get my picture.

We have saturated the horse with our emotions. In silent movies, the hero was identified by having him give a lump of sugar to a horse. The horse provided the only genuineness in the film and was used to certify the actors. The Amish Standardbreds who pull carriages in Central Park have learned what most humans cannot: parallel parking. Their quiet obedience exists in eerie contrast to the agitated city. The horses I saw in the BLM mustang corrals at Rock Springs, Wyoming, whirling, running with every muscle, every vein in sculptural exaggeration, were so alarmed at being swept from the mountain hiding places by government helicopters they seemed bent on mass suicide. But we humans, hanging from the woven wire fence surrounding them, just wanted to be closer to them. My uncles joined the Boston mounted police because it was the only way they could afford to have a horse. Brendan Behan contemptuously defined the Anglo-Irishman as "a Protestant with a horse."

To some people, horses have wings. Horses took the Sioux out of the Minnesota woods. In Montana's Pryor Mountains, they've found horse skeletons with the extra vertebrae of the Spaniards' Moorish steeds, reproachful bones in the hills above the oil refineries. The U.S. Cavalry lost control of the confiscated hunting horses of the Plains Indians whenever buffalo appeared on the horizon: the horses struck free and surrounded the bison though their riders had vanished from their backs forever. The great scholar of the Northern Plains Indians Vern Deusenberry said that the principal point of the Battle of the Little Big Horn was that it was the end of the buffalo culture. It was also the end of the completely free-roaming horsemen of North America, and maybe of the world.

In the American West, the horse is considered part of a sacred birthright even though the native west-erner is no more likely to be a horseman than is an Ohioan or a New Yorker. In the case of populous western states like Texas, he is perhaps less likely. Here in Montana, the most effete native condo dweller will chuckle at an out-of-stater on a horse. But a lover of horses has nothing to prove and no expertise to reveal. It is important that we find animals to love, and that is the end of the story.

It is bootless to argue for the horse in terms of his usefulness. By modern pragmatic standards, the Sarmatians of the ancient Hungarian plains are the only people to have utilized horses fully: they rode them, ate them, drank their blood, made armor out of their hooves, and sacrificed them to their gods.

It is not the duty of the horse to be a biofeedback mechanism for yearning humans; yet it is remarkable how consistently people with horses claim to have learned much about themselves through them. Certainly, the management of a horse will give you a rapid evaluation of your patience, your powers of concentration, and your ability to hold on to delicate ideas for sustained periods of time.

My own horsemanship is peculiar to the country I ride in and the technical limitations of my riding. I can only respect, ignorantly and from afar, the refinements of English riding, fox hunting, jumping, dressage. I know nothing important about them beyond that they

Jimmy Jarrell, ORO Ranch, Arizona.

must not be easy to master. I will go a long way to watch real stadium jumpers and, because my daughter Annie rides them, reining horses. I am particularly interested in the bridle horses of California. Theirs is an ancient art conveyed from the time of Spanish rule and there is a solemn romance about these horses with their swan necks, their Santa Barbara Spanish bridles, their lightning quickness, and the steady whir of the rollers in their bits.

The country available to me permits me to ride farther than anyone is likely to wish to take a horse. I can go to Wyoming from my home in Montana without crossing a road, and I have hundreds of square miles of easily accessed wild foothills. I am a wanderer in any case but I prefer inarticulate companionship. Horses and dogs are ideal and I often go with both. The biggest limitation for dogs in my region is the prevalence of rattlesnakes in the warm months. Despite precaution, all of my dogs have been bitten by them, and all have recovered. The greatest safety for a dog in snake country at the 45th parallel is to be larger than forty pounds; beyond this size it is nearly impossible for a snake to kill one. Actually, horses are in greater danger, as they are sometimes bitten in the nose while grazing: when their passages close, they suffocate because they are unable to breathe through their mouths. Native horses are alert to snakes and I have several times had them abruptly sidepass in the backcountry; it is only when I looked behind us and saw the coiled reptile that I understood the meaning of the sudden movement. My wonderful old mare Sunday Bomb could see a snake from a half mile. The horses we haven't raised have come from Texas and they are well up on snake. They always see them before I do.

I have gone up a mountain trail on a horse, after a year's absence, and had the horse snort and stare in suspicion at a place where a tree has been removed since the horse's last visit, a tree among millions. The phenomenal alertness to space, shape, smell, and light amount to a kind of capacity, if you are unwilling to call it intelligence, beyond the human.

Forty years ago I came off a wild, stormy mountain in the middle of the night in Wyoming. I had no idea where I was, could not even see the ground. The horse took me home. The only thing I can remember was the sense of complete isolation, the horse's shoes sparking beneath me on the granite rocks, and the quiet arrival without a stumble to disturb our passage.

Training a horse then becomes an exploration of the horse's capacity for logic and muscle memory, logic being little more than doing this to avoid that. Trained performance horses are frequently loped for hours before the competition so that all they have left is muscle memory and they are unlikely to get chaotic personal ideas that send them off pattern, at least in human terms. For example, we require cutting horses to stop and turn on their haunches. It is our theory that this is the best way to hold and turn with a cow. It's probably not true. Buffalo and other wild cattle throw their rear quarters around and turn on their front ends. A model of speed and efficiency, the Argentine polo horse turns on his front end. The old "Texas style" polo horse that turns on his hindquarters is a thing of the past: his method of turning around was judged in-efficient. A cutting horse under pressure or otherwise anxious is liable to forget the enforcement of the human idea and turn on his front end; therefore, he is galloped to a state of weariness, whereupon such big ideas do not occur. It is well to understand that this sort of turnaround simply looks right to us. More legiti-mately, a horse turning on its rear end is far easier to ride and less likely to spill with its rider. But we compel the horse to see it our way.

The quiet, circumspect horseman makes every movement and even every thought around a green horse a building block of restraint and confidence. The best horsemen are quiet and consistent, firmly kind, and, from the horse's point of view, good listen-ers. An even temper is essential. Horses are capable of doing repetitive, annoying things, all of which can

be corrected by a knowledgeable horseman who is patient enough to know that the correction may have to go on in very thin layers, like good varnish. Once when I watched Buster Welch, a cutting-horse trainer of whom I will have more to say, schooling my horse Sugar, I was surprised to see him let her drop her shoulder into her turn on the right side, producing a lunging and ineffective turnaround. "Aren't you going to ask her to quit that?" I asked. "Yes," said Buster, "but not all at once."

He knew how much she could absorb. Asking a horse to absorb more than it is capable of results in the excess being translated into anxiety. Anxiety in a horse can spread like a virus. Once it has, it sets the training back severely. Every trainer of dogs and horses knows that a year's work can be lost in a single moment of anger. It is decidedly better to err on the side of asking too little. The greatest error in training horses lies in not showing up for work often enough and trying to accomplish too much when you do.

In his disquisition on horsemanship, Xenophon, the Greek soldier-historian, emphasized patience and kindness in training the horse—"Never deal with him when you are in a fit of passion"—as the only approach that produces a finished and reliable horse, by which he meant a war horse, intended to carry a cuirassed rider into the chaos of armed strife. A horse trained

Bob Wroten, Box 4 Ranch, Oregon.

Small Surrey Team, Welch Ranch, Texas.

for this was treated with the careful feeding and grooming—including the provision of a special sandbox in which to roll—of the most pampered 4-H pony and all toward a mount upon whom one's life must depend. Xenophon's advice has not lost its usefulness in twenty-four hundred years. What he knew was based on long hours on horseback; in one war, he traveled three thousand miles on his horse, fighting much of the way. Under such circumstances horse and rider would have few secrets from each other and it is heartening that Xenophon's conviction was one of deep respect.

For everyday riding, I require a surefooted horse. Some otherwise good horses, and frequently arena horses, are not particularly surefooted in the hills. They can improve, but it is better if they grew up running in rough country. Surefootedness is important to me because I often ride alone, I get into some pinched spots, and I don't wear a helmet. Moreover, it is not a pleasure to ride a stumbling, wooden-footed horse who threatens life and limb in hard country. Ideally, a ranch horse ought to do a job, but I ride far more than ranch work requires. Buster Welch feels that a horse should always be ridden with a purpose, and if there isn't one then the rider should make one up: pick out a windmill on the horizon and ride straight to it. I'm not always successful in remembering this and sometimes

go where the horse feels like going or just wander around looking for birds. However, horses definitely respond to this purposeful riding. I have ridden both field-trail dog horses and mustanging horses, and their drive to meet their objectives, to follow the hunt or to surmount a far hill to improve the view of the action, is something that comes right up through the seat of the rider's pants. Those who have not experienced a horse urgently going somewhere are unaware of their real physical capacity. That is why runaways are so blinding, so explosive. A runaway is far more dangerous than a downright bucking bronc as he becomes intoxicated by his speed and his adrenaline is transformed to rocket fuel.

If you ride in the backcountry alone, you also want a horse that will not come undone if a two-hundred-pound mule deer sails out from under you when you are pushing through the brush. Or, worse, a ten-bird covey of noisy little partridges. I have had some nastily thrilling experiences on arena-contest horses making their first rural rides, experiences that make the hyper-bole about sitting on a keg of dynamite seem plausi-ble. A good country horse should let you hang all sorts of things on the saddle—binoculars, a check cord for your dog, a slicker—and should not have any obvious fears, like that of moving water. Some young horses will break in two when wind blows their tails up under them; some boil over with fear at the sight of anything new. A friend of mine who suffered a stroke and spent a couple of months in northern Montana at a rehabilitation center said the place was full of head-injured horsemen. Riding horses is not the place for baseless courage or heroism. A kind of earned confidence is what is required, though it may run against the institutional inanity that validates foolhardy behavior. I have often noticed that good horsemen are like good sailors, meticulously and quietly tending to one detail after another, all to keep things running smoothly and safely. Once when I was watching Buster train horses, I sat crossways on my saddle, my knee crooked over the saddle horn, as was my habit. Buster stopped his training, rode over to me, and said, "Don't sit that way. It's dangerous." I don't do it anymore.

It is a pleasant thing to have a horse that will ground-tie, though the adage that a ground-tied horse is a loose horse is probably best kept firmly in mind. Some very fine horses will not stay with you if turned loose; they go home to their friends. Herd instinct is a constant magnetism, the early stages of what, in its more annoying form, is called "barn sour." My young mare Sass is the sort that will stay with me. She has no insecurity and is happy to be with me on an adventure. She loves to graze and, so far, it appears that

when I drop the reins, she will stay near. Most, however, will step on the reins and break them, sooner or later, then wander off. I hate losing nice, broken-in, pliant reins and prefer to let the horse drag a halter rope, which will usually cause a departing horse to stumble enough that it can be caught; but smart older horses learn to drag the rope to one side and can even lope that way. I have seen southern horsemen tie a cotton scale weight to their lead shank, a weight they must carry on the saddle betweentimes—usually a trooper's saddle with all sorts of handy rings—and this works quite well. Another method is to put a snap on one rein so that the horse's head can be pulled around and snapped to the D-ring on the back cinch, causing the horse to circle. I have never tried this but I am aware that the horse eventually makes it clear to the rider that it is ready to be trusted and the snap can be dispensed with. There are lots of ways to try these things, but it's important to imagine the consequences of the horse leaving and plan for them.

General tolerance is a great trait in a saddle horse. Our border collie Ella was a sweet and useful dog, usually out of shape for our cattle drive, and it was often necessary to pick her up when she got overheated or exhausted and throw her over the neck of my horse. Ella was quite unabashed when worn out and would come up to my stirrup and stand on

Sorting, ORO Ranch, Arizona.

her hind legs to be picked straight up from the ground and onto the horse, where she amiably took in the cattle drive from a moving and elevated point of observation. My horses went along with this even when she dug in with her claws to keep from toppling over the side. I ride a big, solid gelding named Zip, a great horse to ranch on, and he has had many miles of it. One day my neighbor came over with his three-year-old boy and the little boy demanded to sit on Zip. I lifted him aboard and Zip panicked, snorting, running backward, and preparing to bolt. I was lucky to snatch the child out of the saddle before a disaster occurred. There was a side of Zip I didn't know after hundreds of saddlings.

As between people, there is chemistry, good and bad, between the horse and its rider. We have a ranch gelding named Jack who regards me with anxious suspicion; he slings his head willfully when my wife rides and would prefer going to the barn. The last time I saw my daughter Annie riding him, she was standing on his bare back sailing along under the willow trees, both of them pictures of contented absorption. They have treated each other with benign mutual acceptance from the first moment they met. It happens.

As I have gotten older I have grown less interested in contests for horses and more interested in horses in general. I am very interested in untrained horses, such as yearlings and two-year-olds. There are few things more exciting than releasing a band of young horses from a corral where they have been confined for some time into open space and watching the explosion of movement as these meteors take on open country. This is sufficiently intoxicating to them that one must anticipate the collisions that they, in their understandable euphoria, sometimes fail to take into account. In Montana, wire cuts are called "education marks" but many a good horse has caused its own death in barbed wire and it must be watched vigilantly where horses are held.

On our somewhat marginal cattle ranch, the greatest pleasure is in moving cattle horseback at spring turnout, changing pastures throughout the grass season, and the fall roundup. Some horses have a special aptitude for this work, moving steadily, anticipating herd quitters, willing to plunge into bad places to flush out cattle. When cattle are strung out in front of the horses for a long move, some of the drover sorcery can be felt, some of the enchantment I feel driving home from town when I pass the sign to the west of my ranch, OPEN RANGE. There's little of that left in the West but it may still account for most of the interest. There is an almost Homeric quality about the open-range books, Andy Adams's *Log of a Cowboy* and Teddy "Blue" Abbott's *We Pointed Them North*, that is absent in the literature of the ranch. The avalanche of farm-and-ranch memoirs that pour, because of lack of general interest in them, from tax-supported university presses are mostly dull. The story possibilities of enclosed land are limited. The open range, the open sea, the open sky, the open wounds of the heart, that's where writers shine.

William Cobbett's *Rural Rides* wouldn't have its charm and power without the horse. The little stallion on Tolstoy's *Master and Man* is one of the best characters in the story and the greatest sacrifice to Tolstoy's tragic art. The boys that take the band of horses to the country during fly season in Turgenev's immortal *Bezhin Meadow* share the companionship and destiny of their charges. The mastery of Beryl Markham's horsemanship is the capacity that gives the flight and exploration of *West with the Night* its resonance. Hemingway's curious lack of interest in the horse, his insouciance at the goring of the picadors' horses and the replacement of their bowels with sawdust that they may continue the job, causes me to wonder at him anew. Perhaps he might have taken a lesson from Faulkner, who kept a few apples in his old coat for his horses and mules.

Indeed, to go forth with an animal, a dowager with her poodle, a hunter with his setter, a falconer with his hawk, a pirate with his parrot, is to enlarge one's affect such that the whole is greater than the sum of its parts. Poor horsemanship consists in suggesting that man and horse are separate. A horseman afoot is a wingless, broken thing, tyrannized by gravity. I have often been astounded after a great performance by horse and rider to encounter the rider afterward, a crumpled figure, negligible in every discernible way, a defeated, aging little man; or a crone, where moments ago a demon or a fire queen filled us with obsessive attention. And even the horses are turned into weary pensioners as, with empty saddles and lowered heads, they are led to their stalls to rest. For that burst of poetry, horse and rider have one another to thank.

Men's achievements have been enlarged by horses almost as if the animals' plangent silence implied what could never be merely said. Napoleon's famous horse Marengo, George Washington's gray Arab Magnolia, Grant's horse Cincinnati, Lee's horse Traveller, and Comanche, the one horse to survive the Battle of the Little Big Horn, were regarded with awe because horses, even the bones of horses, remember everything. Nothing focused the nation's mourning like the riderless black horse in the funeral cortege of John Kennedy.

At the Battle of Waterloo, men formed squares into which the wounded were brought for medical care. At the height of the battle, in the madness of the

Joe, Bob, Mary Lou, and Michael William Coffelt, Rafter Cross Ranch, California.

cannonading and death, the riderless horses of the cavalry, the caisson horses of the slaughtered gun crews attempted to penetrate the squares to be saved by the humans. And in the First World War, men subjected to unparalleled mayhem were stricken more by the plight of the horses than anything else. There is a special grief for the innocent caught up in mankind's murderous follies. The idea of horses with their self-absorbed innocence embroiled in war is deeply disquieting. In Andrei Makine's memoir of Siberian life, *Dream of My Russian Summers*, images of riderless but completely equipped White Russian cavalry horses, some with sabers swinging from the points at which they were plunged, running wild through a depopulated landscape suggest the fury of human conflict that has surpassed human control.

Hunting on horseback, following bird dogs through an oak forest, which I have done with indescribable pleasure and a hint of self-satisfaction perhaps at the very picture I imagined myself conveying, seems a coherent activity in which man and horse and dogs, birds and forest coalesce into something of duration. Add one motor scooter to this picture, or even the man trotting along on his inadequate legs, and you get something much reduced and thoroughly unbeautiful. From the time of the Greeks and, unrecorded, certainly before, it has been an explicit matter that mankind must have beauty to live.

—THOMAS McGUANE

Gazer, Stucky Ranch, Montana.

Allan Fullmer, Flat Mountain Quarter Horse Ranch, Alaska.
Overleaf: Justin Fields, Fields Cattle Co., California.

WHEN I KNELT BY THE FOAL, AN EXQUISITE SORREL FILLY, HER HEAD NODDED UP AND DOWN AND SHE MADE SEVERAL ATTEMPTS TO STAND. HER TINY BLACK HOOVES WERE JUST BEGINNING TO HARDEN.

—THOMAS McGUANE

IT ISN'T REALLY SUMMER until the shelter belt on the east side of the corrals leafs out. That makes all the difference because it blocks the sun in the first corral. It is also the time when, if you sit in the ancient Crow vision-quest site on the western side of the ranch, you will see the sun rise at the center of the valley in a remarkable suggestion of the first light of the world.

A FOAL

I had three mares confined. Two had already had their colts and the third, my adored quarter horse LuLu, was three weeks late and very uncomfortable. The saddle horses, five geldings, including two venerated pensioners in their twenties, stayed close to the corrals in their pasture because they were interested in these births and had proved to be doting uncles over the years. But in the summertime at first light, they were usually lying down asleep in the sun. Nothing moved, not even their tails, because it was still too cool for flies.

I usually get up early and head to the bunkhouse, where I work. I don't always go straight in there as I try to suggest by my brisk departure. I worried that in that building, hunched over a legal pad still in the trance of sleep, I might feel irony was required and it was much too early for that; though in the early quiet, it is often to big issues one's mind wanders, guilt at all this tranquility, the

CS Ranch, New Mexico.

feeling that I and my work had been diminished by thirty years of rusticating among the Missouri's smallest headwaters. At such times, I console myself with some literary anecdote like Mencken's remark that he didn't care how well Willa Cather wrote, he wasn't interested in anything that happened in Nebraska, a remark that blew up in Mencken's face like an exploding cigar. Or, I think of the ways Montaigne got everyone to visit him in the boondocks. And so on and so forth. I was carrying my coffee. A small river whispers around the edge of the yard and down behind the barn, a sparkling freestone river that springs from a mountain range I can see to the south. Its height changes daily according to melt-off and storms in the mountains, events I couldn't detect; but I can see the dark rings around the stones when the river is falling, the shells of transforming stoneflies, the dart of yellow warblers crossing the river to their willow nests.

LuLu had not been happy, not eating, strangely unimpressed by the snacks I kept in my coat, and after two weeks her broodiness had infected me. When I reached under to feel her taut udder, its heat and softness were pronounced; she pretended to lift a leg toward me with an annoyed grunt but I knew it was because she was sore. Her foal liked one side of her body one day and the next was on the other, pushing a knee around the side of LuLu's stomach.

LuLu laid her ears back close to her head at this provocation. It did seem that the nipples had faintly exuded some wax, which, just ahead of the colostrum, could mean imminent birth. LuLu was the tenderest of animals, though in her days as a cutting horse she could astonish with her bursts of speed and hard, sliding stops. She mourned for six weeks when a friend of hers, a cat, went to another ranch to mouse. So her stoniness toward me at this late hour of her confinement was disquieting.

One morning, I made my accustomed feint toward the place of work and irony, and went to the corrals. The geldings were asleep in the pasture, except for the most avuncular of them, Lucky Bottom 79. LuLu no longer consorted with the mares who already had their colts. Instead, she stood in the shade of the caragana bushes without any movement. She was thinner all right, but she looked alone. I went to her with a chill of fear; the speed of birth in horses is such that things go wrong quickly. But when I was a few paces away, a small head popped up and regarded me; the foal was almost invisible against the ground and LuLu nickered to me. The afterbirth was on the ground a couple of yards away. I lifted it up and inspected it for completeness. Glistening, startlingly heavy, and still warm, the afterbirth was shaped like the bottom of a pair of long underwear with one leg shorter than the other. Any dog worthy of the name, like my three, considers this a windfall of immaculate protein.

When I knelt by the foal, an exquisite sorrel filly, her head nodded up and down and she made several attempts to stand. Her tiny black hooves were just beginning to harden. LuLu buried her nostrils in my hair to reconfirm my identity and let me examine the little horse, who presently heaved herself onto sprawled legs wobbling and erect. Arms around her torso, her coat warm and dry, eyes big as a deer's, the beat of her heart coming through her rib cage as she yearned toward LuLu's udder, I steadied her until the connection was made and I saw the pumping movement in her throat.

A new horse.

—THOMAS McGUANE

Poppy and Moony.